# EASY KETO DIET

## Your Essential Guide to Living the Keto Lifestyle with keto meal and delicious recipes

GW00370790

## BY

## DAVID PHILLIPS

# Contents

## Introduction to a keto diet

The KETO-genic keto diet is a high-fat, adequate-protein, low-starch keto diet that in medication is used basically to get control over troublesome (refractory) epilepsy—this plan empowers the body to consume fats instead of sugars.

A specific level of ketone bodies in the blood produces a state known as ketogenic, and prompts a loss in the chance of epileptic seizures. Around half of the youngsters with epilepsy who have tried this type of eating plan saw all thire seizures drop by at least half. The lasting effect is significant in the wake of stopping this eating plan.

Some proof shows that adults with epilepsy may profit by this eating plan and that a less rigorous method, such as an adjusted Atkins keto diet, is comparatively successful. Potential reactions may incorporate clogging, elevated cholesterol, development easing back, and kidney stones.

## Keto Recipes

# Egg-Meat Rolls

**Prep time:** 15 minutes
**Cooking time:** 8 minute
**Servings:** 6

## Ingredients:

- ½ cup almond flour
- ¼ cup water
- 1 teaspoon salt
- 1 egg
- 7 oz. finely ground beef
- 1 teaspoon paprika to taste
- 1 teaspoon finely ground black pepper
- 1 tablespoon extra virgin olive oil

## Directions:

1. Heat the water until it starts to boil.
2. And then mix together the almond flour with the salt and slowly stir it.
3. Add the boiling water and whisk it carefully until the mixture is homogenous.
4. And then knead the smooth and soft dough.
5. Leave the dough.
6. And then, mix together the finely ground beef with the paprika to taste and finely ground black pepper.
7. Mix the mixture well and move it to the pan.
8. Roast the meat mixture for 5 minutes on the medium heat. Slowly stir it frequently.
9. And then beat the egg in the meat mixture and scramble it.
10. Cook the finely ground beef mixture for 4 minutes more.
11. And then roll the dough and cut it into the 6 squares.

12.     Place the finely ground beef mixture in the each square.

13.     Roll the squares to make the dough sticks.

14.     Coat the dough sticks with the extra virgin olive oil.

15.     And then, place the prepared dough sticks in the air fryer basket.

16.     Heat the air fryer to 350 F and place the egg-meat rolls there.

17.     Cook the dish for 8 minutes.

18.     When the egg-meat rolls are cooked – move them directly to the serving plates.

19.     Enjoy!

**Nutrition:** calories 150, fat 9.6, fiber 1.2, carbs 2.5, protein 13

# Classic Egg Rolls

**Prep time:** 10 minutes
**Cooking time:** 8 minutes
**Servings:** 4

## Ingredients:

- 6 tablespoon coconut flour
- ½ teaspoon salt
- 1 teaspoon paprika to taste
- 1 teaspoon butter
- 4 eggs
- 1 teaspoon chives
- 1 tablespoon extra virgin olive oil
- 2 tablespoon water, boiled, hot

## Directions:

1. Place the coconut flour in the small bowl.
2. Add salt and hot boiled water.
3. Mix it well and knead the soft dough.
4. And then, leave the dough to rest.
5. And then, break the eggs into the small bowl.

6.  Add the chives and paprika to taste.

7.  Whisk it up with the help of the hand whisker.

8.  And then toss the butter in the pan and Heat it well.

9.  Pour the egg mixture in the melted butter in the shape of the pancake.

10.  And then cook the egg pancake for 1 minute from the each side.

11.  And then, remove the cooked egg pancake and cleave it.

12.  Roll the prepared dough and cut it into the 4 squares.

13.  Place the cleaved eggs in the dough squares and roll them in the shape of the sticks.

14.  And then brush the egg rolls with the extra virgin olive oil.

15.  Heat the air fryer to 355 F.

16.  Place the egg rolls in the basket and move the basket in the air fryer.

17. Cook the dish for 8 minutes.
18. After the due time the rolls will get light brown color.
19. Serve the dish hot.
20. Enjoy1

**Nutrition:** calories 148, fat 10, fiber 4.7, carbs 8.2, protein 7.1

# Breakfast Sausages

**Prep time:** 15 minutes
**Cooking time:** 12 minutes
**Servings:** 6

## Ingredients:

- 7 oz. finely ground chicken
- 7 oz. finely ground pork
- 1 teaspoon diced garlic
- 1 teaspoon salt
- ½ teaspoon nutmeg
- 1 teaspoon extra virgin olive oil
- 1 tablespoon almond flour
- 1 egg
- 1 teaspoon chili flakes
- 1 teaspoon finely ground coriander

## Directions:

1. Mix together the finely ground chicken and finely ground pork together in the small bowl.
2. Beat the egg in the mixture.
3. And then Mix it well with the help of the spoon.

4. And then, coat the meat mixture with the diced garlic, salt, nutmeg, almond flour, chili flakes, and finely ground coriander.

5. Mix it well to make the smooth texture of the finely ground meat.

6. Heat the air fryer to 360 F.

7. Make the medium sausages from the finely ground meat mixture.

8. Spray the air fryer tray with the extra virgin olive oil inside.

9. And then place the prepared sausages in the air fryer basket and place it in the air fryer.

10. Cook the sausages for 6 minutes.

11. And then, turn the sausages into the second side and cook them for 6 minutes more.

12. After the due time and the sausages are cooked – let them chill little.

13. Serve and taste!

**Nutrition:** calories 156, fat 7.5, fiber 0.6, carbs 1.3, protein 20.2

# Breakfast Blackberry Muffins

**Prep time:** 15 minutes
**Cooking time:** 10 minutes
**Servings:** 5

## Ingredients:

- 1 teaspoon apple cider vinegar
- 1 cup almond flour
- 4 tablespoon butter
- 6 tablespoon almond milk
- 1 teaspoon baking soda
- 3 oz. blackberry
- ½ teaspoon salt
- 3 teaspoon stevia
- 1 teaspoon vanilla extract

## Directions:

1. Place the almond flour in the mixing small bowl.
2. Add the baking soda, salt, stevia, and vanilla extract.
3. And then, add butter, almond milk, and apple cider vinegar.
4. Smash the blackberries gently and add them to the almond flour mixture.
5. Slowly stir it carefully with the help of the fork until the mass is homogeneous.
6. And then, leave the muffin mixture for 5 minutes in warm place.
7. Heat the air fryer to 400 F.
8. Prepare the muffin forms.
9. Pour the dough in the muffin forms. Fill only ½ part of each muffin form.
10. When the air fryer is Heated – place the muffing forms with the filling in the air fryer basket. Close the air fryer.
11. Cook the muffins for 10 minutes.
12. After the due time – remove the muffins from the air fryer basket.
13. Chill them until they are warm.
14. Serve them and enjoy!

**Nutrition:** calories 165, fat 16.4, fiber 1.9, carbs 4, protein 2

# Light Egg Soufflé

**Prep time:** 8 minutes
**Cooking time:** 8 minutes
**Servings:** 2

## Ingredients:

- 2 eggs
- 2 tablespoon heavy cream
- 1 tablespoon dried parsley
- ¼ teaspoon finely ground chili pepper
- ¼ teaspoon salt

## Directions:

1. Heat the air fryer to 391 F.
2. And then, break the eggs into the small bowl and add the heavy cream.

3. Whisk the mixture carefully until you get the smooth liquid texture.
4. And then, coat the egg mixture with the dried parsley, finely ground chili pepper, and salt.
5. Mix it well with the help of the spoon.
6. And then take 2 ramekins and pour the soufflé mixture there.
7. Place the ramekins in the air fryer basket and cook for 8 minutes.
8. After the due time and the soufflé is prepared – remove the ramekins from the air fryer basket and chill for 2-3 minutes.
9. Serve the dish and enjoy!

**Nutrition:** calories 116, fat 9.9, fiber 0.1, carbs 0.9, protein 5.9

# Chia Pudding

**Prep time:** 10 minutes
**Cooking time:** 4 minutes
**Servings:** 7

**Ingredients:**
- 1 cup chia seeds
- 1 cup coconut milk
- 1 teaspoon stevia
- 1 tablespoon coconut
- 1 teaspoon butter

**Directions:**
1. Take the small ramekins and place the chia seeds there.
2. Add the coconut milk and stevia.
3. Slowly stir the mixture gently with the help of the teaspoon.
4. And then, add coconut and butter.
5. Place the chia seeds pudding in the air fryer tray and Heat the air fryer to 360 F.
6. Cook the chia pudding for 4 minutes.
7. After the due time – remove the ramekins with the chia pudding

from the air fryer and chill it for 4 minutes.

8. And then, slowly stir each chia pudding serving with the help of the teaspoon and serve it.
9. Enjoy!

**Nutrition:** calories 204, fat 16.4, fiber 10.2, carbs 12.2, protein 4.8

# Keto Morning Pizza

**Prep time:** 10 minutes
**Cooking time:** 11 minutes
**Servings:** 6

## Ingredients:
- 6 oz. Cheddar cheese, minced
- 5 oz. Parmesan cheese, minced
- 1 tomato
- ¼ onion
- 1 teaspoon paprika to taste
- ½ teaspoon dried oregano
- ½ teaspoon salt
- ½ cup almond flour
- 1 egg

- 4 tablespoon water
- 1 teaspoon extra virgin olive oil

**Directions:**

1. Beat the egg in the small bowl and whisk it with the help of the hand whisker.
2. And then, add the almond flour and water. Mix the mixture up carefully Then knead the non-sticky dough.
3. Roll the dough into the thin circle.
4. Heat the air fryer to 355 F.
5. Spray the air fryer tray with the extra virgin olive oil and place the pizza crust there.
6. Cook it for 1 minute.
7. And then, remove the air fryer tray from the air fryer.
8. Cut the tomato and dice the onion.
9. Coat the pizza crust with the diced onion and cut tomato.
10. And then place the minced Cheddar cheese and Parmesan cheese over the cut tomatoes.
11. Coat the pizza with salt, paprika to taste, and dried oregano.

12. Place the pizza back in the air fryer and cook it for 10 minutes.
13. After the due time and the pizza is prepared – cut it into the servings and serve!

**Nutrition:** calories 226, fat 17.2, fiber 0.7, carbs 2.9, protein 16.3

# Buffalo Cauliflower

**Prep time:** 10 minutes
**Cooking time:** 15 minutes
**Servings:** 5

## Ingredients:

- 8 oz. cauliflower
- 6 tablespoon almond flour
- 1 teaspoon chili pepper
- 1 teaspoon cayenne pepper
- 1 teaspoon finely ground black pepper
- 1 tomato
- 1 teaspoon diced garlic
- ½ teaspoon salt

- 1 teaspoon extra virgin olive oil

**Directions:**

1. Wash the cauliflower carefully and separate it into the medium florets.
2. Coat the cauliflower florets with the salt.
3. And then, cleave the tomato roughly and move it to the blender.
4. Blend it well.
5. And then add the chili pepper, cayenne pepper, finely ground black pepper, and diced garlic.
6. Blend the mixture.
7. And then Heat the air fryer to 350 F.
8. Coat the air fryer basket with the extra virgin olive oil inside.
9. Coat the cauliflower florets with the blended tomato mixture generously.
10. And then, coat the cauliflower florets in the almond flour.
11. Place the coated cauliflower florets in the air fryer basket and cook the dish for 15 minutes.

12. Shake the cauliflower florets each 4 minutes.
13. When the cauliflower is prepared – it will have light brown color.
14. Move it to the serving plates.
15. Enjoy!

**Nutrition:** calories 217, fat 17.9, fiber 5.1, carbs 10.8, protein 8.4

# Pork Breakfast Sticks

**Prep time:** 15 minutes
**Cooking time:** 10 minutes
**Servings:** 4

## Ingredients:

- 1 teaspoon dried basil
- ¼ teaspoon finely ground ginger
- 1 teaspoon nutmeg
- 1 teaspoon oregano
- 1 teaspoon apple cider vinegar
- 1 teaspoon paprika to taste
- 10 oz. pork fillet
- ½ teaspoon salt
- 1 tablespoon extra virgin olive oil
- 5 oz. Parmesan, minced

## Directions:

1. Cut the pork fillet into the thick strips.
2. And then mix together the finely ground ginger, nutmeg, oregano, paprika to taste, and salt in the shallow small bowl. Slowly stir it.
3. And then, coat the pork strips with the spice mixture.

4. Coat the meat with the apple cider vinegar.
5. Heat the air fryer to 380 F.
6. Coat the air fryer basket with the extra virgin olive oil inside and place the pork strips (sticks) there.
7. Cook the dish for 5 minutes.
8. And then, turn the pork sticks to another side and cook for 4 minutes more.
9. And then cover the pork sticks with the minced Parmesan and cook the dish for 1 minute more.
10. Remove the pork sticks from the air fryer and serve them immediately. The cheese will be soft during the serving.
11. Enjoy!

**Nutrition:** calories 315, fat 20.4, fiber 0.5, carbs 2.2, protein 31.3

# Keto Bacon

**Prep time:** 8 minutes
**Cooking time:** 10 minutes
**Servings:** 4

## Ingredients:

- 8 oz. bacon
- ½ teaspoon dried oregano
- ½ teaspoon salt
- ½ teaspoon finely ground black pepper
- ½ teaspoon finely ground thyme
- 4 oz. Cheddar cheese

## Directions:

1. Cut the bacon and rub it with the dried oregano, salt, finely ground

black pepper, and finely ground thyme from the each side.

2. Leave the bacon for 2-3 minutes to make it soak the spices.
3. And then, Heat the air fryer to 360 F.
4. Place the cut bacon in the air fryer rack and cook it for 5 minutes.
5. And then, turn the cut bacon to another side and cook it for 5 minutes more.
6. And then, shred Cheddar cheese.
7. When the bacon is prepared – coat it with the minced cheese and cook for 30 seconds more.
8. And then move the cooked bacon to the plates.
9. Enjoy the breakfast immediately!

**Nutrition:** calories 423, fat 33.1, fiber 0.2, carbs 1.5, protein 28.1

# Cheese Tots

**Prep time:** 12 minutes
**Cooking time:** 3 minutes
**Servings:** 5

**Ingredients:**

- 8 oz. mozzarella balls
- 1 egg
- ½ cup coconut flakes
- ½ cup almond flour
- 1 teaspoon thyme
- 1 teaspoon finely ground black pepper
- 1 teaspoon paprika to taste

**Directions:**

1. Beat the egg in the small bowl and whisk it.
2. And then, mix together the coconut flour with the thyme, finely ground black pepper, and paprika to taste. Slowly stir it carefully.
3. Then coat Mozzarella balls with the coconut flakes.

4. And then, move the balls to the whisked egg mixture And then coat them in the almond flour mixture.
5. Place Mozzarella balls in the freezer for 5 minutes.
6. And then, Heat the air fryer to 400 F.
7. Place the frozen cheese balls in the heated air fryer and cook them for 3 minutes.
8. After the due time – remove the cheese tots from the air fryer basket and chill them for 2 minutes.
9. Serve the dish!

**Nutrition:** calories 166, fat 12.8, fiber 1.4, carbs 2.8, protein 9.5

# Egg Cups with Bacon

**Prep time:** 10 minutes
**Cooking time:** 15 minutes
**Servings:** 4

## Ingredients:
- 4 eggs

- 6 oz. bacon
- ¼ teaspoon salt
- ½ teaspoon dried dill
- ½ teaspoon paprika to taste
- 1 tablespoon butter

**Directions:**

1. Beat the eggs in the small small bowl.
2. And then, add salt, dried dill, and a some paprika to taste. Mix the egg mixture carefully.
3. And then spread 4 small ramekins with the butter.
4. Cut the bacon and place it in the prepared small ramekins in the shape of cups.
5. And then pour the egg mixture in each ramekin with bacon.
6. Pre heat the Air Fryer to 360 F.
7. Cook the dish for 15 minutes.
8. Remove the egg cups from the Air Fryer and serve them.
9. Enjoy!

**Nutrition:** calories 319, fat 25.1, fiber 0.1, carbs 1.2, protein 21.4

# Eggs in Avocado Boards

**Prep time:** 8 minutes
**Cooking time:** 15 minutes
**Servings:** 2

## Ingredients:

- 1 avocado, pitted
- ¼ teaspoon turmeric
- ¼ teaspoon finely ground black pepper
- ¼ teaspoon salt
- 2 eggs
- 1 teaspoon butter
- ¼ teaspoon flax seeds

## Directions:

1.    Take the shallow small bowl and mix together the turmeric, finely ground black pepper, salt, and flax seeds together. And shake it gently to make homogeneous.

2.    And then cut the avocado into 2 parts.

3.    Beat the eggs in the separate small bowls and Coat the eggs with the spice mixture.

4.    And then place these eggs in the avocado halves and  Place the avocado boards in the Air Fryer.

5.    Set the Air Fryer to 355 F and close it.

6.    Cook the dish for 15 minutes.

7.    Serve the breakfast immediately!

**Nutrition:** calories 288, fat 26, fiber 6.9, carbs 9.4, protein 7.6

# Morning Ham Hash

**Prep time:** 10 minutes
**Cooking time:** 10 minutes
**Servings:** 3

## Ingredients:

- 5 oz. Parmesan
- 10 oz. ham
- 1 tablespoon butter
- ½ onion
- 1 teaspoon finely ground black pepper
- 1 egg
- 1 teaspoon paprika to taste

## Directions:

1. Shred Parmesan cheese.

2.  Cut the ham into the small strips.

3.  Peel the onion and dice it smoothly.

4.  Beat the egg in the small bowl and whisk it. And then Add the ham strips, butter, diced onion, butter and coat the mixture with the finely ground black pepper and paprika to taste.

5.  Mix it well.

6.  Heat Air Fryer to 350 F. And then move the ham mixture into 3 ramekins and coat them with the minced Parmesan cheese.

7.  Place the ramekins in the Heated Air Fryer and cook them for 10 minutes.

8.  Serve the dish!

**Nutrition:** calories 372, fat 23.7, fiber 2.1, carbs 8, protein 33.2

# Cloud Eggs

**Prep time:** 8 minutes
**Cooking time:** 4 minutes
**Servings:** 2

## Ingredients:

- 2 eggs
- 1 teaspoon butter

## Directions:

1.  Separate the eggs into the egg whites and the egg yolks and And then whisk the egg whites

with the help of the hand mixer until you get strong white peaks.

2. And then spread the Air Fryer tray with the butter.

3. Heat the Air Fryer to 300 F.

4. Place the tray in the Air Fryer and cook the cloud eggs for 2 minutes.

5. And then, remove the basket from the Air Fryer, place the egg yolks in the center of each egg cloud, and return the basket back in the Air Fryer.

6. Cook the dish for 2 minutes more. Serve immediately and Enjoy!

**Nutrition:** calories 80, fat 6.3, fiber 0, carbs 0.3, protein 5.6

# Baked Bacon Egg Cups

**Prep time:** 10 minutes
**Cooking time:** 12 minutes
**Servings:** 2

## Ingredients:

- 2 eggs
- 4 oz. bacon
- ¼ teaspoon salt
- ½ teaspoon butter
- 3 oz. Cheddar cheese, minced
- ½ teaspoon cayenne pepper
- ½ teaspoon paprika to taste
- 1 tablespoon chives

**Directions:**

1. Cut the bacon into the tiny pieces and coat it with the salt, cayenne pepper, and paprika to taste and mix it well.

2. And then, spread the ramekins with the butter and beat the eggs there. And then add the minced cheese and chives.

3. And then, place the bacon over the chives.

4. Place the ramekins in the Air Fryer basket and Heat the air fryer to 360 F.

5. Cook the breakfast for 12 minutes.

6. Remove the bacon egg cups from the ramekins carefully.

7. Enjoy!

**Nutrition:** calories 553, fat 43.3, fiber 0.4, carbs 2.3, protein 37.3

# Cauliflower Fritters

**Prep time:** 10 minutes
**Cooking time:** 15 minutes
**Servings:** 4

## Ingredients:

- 1 tablespoon dried dill
- 1 egg
- 1 teaspoon salt
- 10 oz. cauliflower
- 1 tablespoon almond flour
- 1 teaspoon extra virgin olive oil
- 1 tablespoon parsley
- ½ teaspoon finely ground white pepper

## Directions:

1.  Wash the cauliflower carefully and cut it into the small pieces.

2.  And then place the cauliflower in the blender and blend it well. Add egg and blend it for 1 minute.

3.  And then move the blended cauliflower mixture in the small bowl.

4.  Coat it with the salt, dried dill, almond flour, parsley, and finely ground white pepper.

5.  Mix it well carefully with the help of the spoon.

6.  Heat the air fryer to 355 F.

7.  And then coat the air fryer tray with the extra virgin olive oil.

8.  Make the fritters from the cauliflower mixture and place them in the air fryer tray.

9.  Close the air fryer and cook the fritters for 8 minutes.

10.  And then, turn the fritters to another side and cook them for 7 minutes more.

11.  When the fritters are cooked – serve them hot!

12.    Enjoy!

**Nutrition:** calories 54, fat 3.1, fiber 2.1, carbs 4.8, protein 3.3

# Sausage Balls

**Prep time:** 10 minutes
**Cooking time:** 8 minutes
**Servings:** 5

## Ingredients:
- 8 oz. finely ground chicken
- 1 egg white
- 1 tablespoon dried parsley
- ½ teaspoon salt
- ½ teaspoon finely ground black pepper
- 2 tablespoon almond flour
- 1 tablespoon extra virgin olive oil
- 1 teaspoon paprika to taste

## Directions:

1. Whisk the egg white and mix together it with the finely ground chicken.
2. Coat the chicken mixture with the dried parsley and salt.
3. And then, add the finely ground black pepper and paprika to taste.
4. Slowly stir the mass carefully using the spoon.

5. And then make the hands wet and make the small balls from the finely ground chicken mixture.
6. Coat each sausage ball with the almond flour.
7. Heat the air fryer to 380 F.
8. And then spray the air fryer tray with the extra virgin olive oil inside and place the sausage balls there.
9. Cook the dish for 8 minutes.
10. You can turn the balls into another side during the cooking to get the brown color of the each side.
11. Move the cooked sausage balls in the serving plates.
12. Enjoy!

**Nutrition:** calories 180, fat 11.8, fiber 1.5, carbs 2.9, protein 16.3

# Tofu Scramble

**Prep time:** 15 minutes
**Cooking time:** 20 minutes
**Servings:** 5

## Ingredients:
- 10 oz tofu cheese
- 2 eggs
- 1 teaspoon chives
- 1 tablespoon apple cider vinegar

- ½ teaspoon salt
- 1 teaspoon finely ground white pepper
- ¼ teaspoon finely ground coriander

**Directions:**

1. Shred tofu cheese and coat it with the apple cider vinegar, salt, finely ground white pepper, and finely ground coriander.
2. Mix it well and leave for 10 minutes to marinate.
3. And then, Heat the air fryer to 370 F.
4. And then move the marinated minced tofu cheese in the air fryer tray and cook the cheese for 13 minutes.
5. And then, beat the eggs in the small bowl and whisk them.
6. After the due time – pour the egg mixture in the minced tofu cheese and slowly stir it with the help of the spatula well.
7. When the eggs start to be cooked – place the air fryer tray in the air

fryer and cook the dish for 7 minutes more.
8. And then, remove the cooked meal from the air fryer tray and serve it.
9. Enjoy!

**Nutrition:** calories 109, fat 6.7, fiber 1.4, carbs 2.9, protein 11.2

# Hemp Seeds Porridge

**Prep time:** 10 minutes
**Cooking time:** 15 minutes
**Servings:** 3

## Ingredients:

- 2 tablespoon flax seeds
- 4 tablespoon hemp seeds
- 1 tablespoon butter
- ¼ teaspoon salt
- 1 teaspoon stevia
- 7 tablespoon almond milk
- ½ teaspoon finely ground ginger

## Directions:

1. Place the flax seeds and hemp seeds in the air fryer basket.
2. Coat the seeds with the salt and finely ground ginger.
3. Mix together the almond milk and stevia together. Slowly stir the liquid and pour it in the seeds mixture.
4. And then, add butter.

5. Heat the air fryer to 370 F and cook the hemp seeds porridge for 15 minutes.
6. Slowly stir it carefully after 10 minutes of cooking.
7. After the due time – remove the hem porridge from the air fryer tray and chill it for 3 minutes.
8. Move the Hemp Seeds porridge in the serving small bowls.
9. Enjoy!

**Nutrition:** calories 196, fat 18.2, fiber 2.4, carbs 4.2, protein 5.1

# Bacon Scrambled Eggs

**Prep time:** 10 minutes
**Cooking time:** 10 minutes
**Servings:** 4

## Ingredients:

- 6 oz. bacon
- 4 eggs
- 5 tablespoon heavy cream
- 1 tablespoon butter
- 1 teaspoon paprika to taste
- ½ teaspoon nutmeg
- 1 teaspoon salt
- 1 teaspoon finely ground black pepper

## Directions:

1. Cleave the bacon into the small pieces and coat it with salt.
2. Slowly stir the bacon gently and place in the air fryer basket.
3. Cook the cleaved bacon in the Heated to 360 F air fryer for 5 minutes.

4. And then, beat the eggs in the small bowl and whisk them using the hand whisker.
5. Coat the whisked egg mixture with the paprika to taste, nutmeg, and finely ground black pepper.
6. Whisk egg mixture gently again.
7. After the due time – toss the butter in the cleaved bacon and pour the egg mixture.
8. Add the heavy cream and cook it for 2 minutes.
9. And then, slowly stir the mixture with the help of the spatula until you get the scrambled eggs and cook the dish for 3 minutes more.
10.  And then move the cooked bacon scrambled eggs in the serving plates.
11.  Enjoy!

**Nutrition:** calories 387, fat 32.1, fiber 0.4, carbs 2.3, protein 21.9

# Delightful Breakfast Hash

**Prep time:** 8 minutes
**Cooking time:** 8 minutes
**Servings:** 4

## Ingredients:

- 1 zucchini
- 7 oz. bacon, cooked
- 4 oz. Cheddar cheese
- 2 tablespoon butter

- 1 teaspoon salt
- 1 teaspoon finely ground black pepper
- 1 teaspoon paprika to taste
- 1 teaspoon cilantro
- 1 teaspoon finely ground thyme

**Directions:**

1. Cleave the zucchini into the small cubes and coat it with the salt, finely ground black pepper, paprika to taste, cilantro, and finely ground thyme.
2. Heat the air fryer to 400 F and toss the butter in the air fryer tray.
3. Melt it and add the zucchini cubes.
4. Cook the zucchini for 5 minutes.
5. And then, shred Cheddar cheese.
6. After the due time – shake the zucchini cubes carefully and add the cooked bacon.
7. Coat the zucchini mixture with the minced cheese and cook it for 3 minutes more.
8. After the due time – move the breakfast hash in the serving small bowls and slowly stir.
9. Enjoy!

**Nutrition:** calories 445, fat 36.1, fiber 1, carbs 3.5, protein 26.3

# Cheddar Soufflé with Greens

**Prep time:** 10 minutes
**Cooking time:** 8 minutes
**Servings:** 4

## Ingredients:
- 5 oz. Cheddar cheese, minced
- 3 eggs
- 4 tablespoon heavy cream
- 1 tablespoon chives
- 1 tablespoon dill
- 1 teaspoon parsley
- ½ teaspoon finely ground thyme

## Directions:
1. Break the eggs into the small bowl and whisk them carefully.
2. And then, add the heavy cream and whisk it for 10 seconds more.
3. And then add the chives, dill, parsley, and finely ground thyme.
4. Coat the egg mixture with the minced cheese and slowly stir it.
5. Move the egg mixture in 4 ramekins and place the ramekins in the air fryer basket.

6. Heat the air fryer to 390 F and cook the soufflé for 8 minutes.
7. After the due time and the soufflé is prepared – chill it well.
8. Enjoy!

**Nutrition:** calories 244, fat 20.6, fiber 0.2, carbs 1.7, protein 13.5

# Bacon Biscuits

**Prep time:** 15 minutes
**Cooking time:** 10 minutes
**Servings:** 6

## Ingredients:

- 1 egg
- 4 oz. bacon, cooked
- 1 cup almond flour
- ½ teaspoon baking soda
- 1 tablespoon apple cider vinegar
- 3 tablespoon butter
- 4 tablespoon heavy cream
- 1 teaspoon dried oregano

## Directions:

1. Beat the egg in the small bowl and whisk it.
2. Cleave the cooked bacon into the small cubes and add it in the whisked egg.
3. And then coat the mixture with the baking soda and apple cider vinegar.
4. Add the heavy cream and dried oregano. Slowly stir it.

5. And then, add butter and almond flour.
6. Mix it well with the help of the hand mixer.
7. When you get the smooth and liquid batter – the dough is prepared.
8. Heat the air fryer to 400 F.
9. Pour the batter dough into the muffin molds.
10. When the air fryer is heated – place the muffin forms in the air fryer basket and cook them for 10 minutes.
11. After the due time and the muffins are prepared – remove them from the air fryer.
12. Chill the muffins till the room temperature.
13. Serve!

**Nutrition:** calories 226, fat 20.5, fiber 0.6, carbs 1.8, protein 9.2

# Keto Frittata

**Prep time:** 10 minutes
**Cooking time:** 15 minutes
**Servings:** 6

## Ingredients:

- 6 eggs
- 1/3 cup heavy cream
- 1 tomato
- 1/2 onion
- 1 tablespoon butter
- 1 teaspoon salt
- 1 tablespoon dried oregano
- 6 oz. Parmesan
- 1 teaspoon chili pepper

## Directions:

1. Beat the eggs in the air fryer tray and whisk them with the help of the hand whisker.
2. And then, cleave the tomato and dice the onion.
3. Add the vegetables to the egg mixture.
4. And then pour the heavy cream.

5. Coat the liquid mixture with the butter, salt, dried oregano, and chili pepper.
6. And then shred Parmesan cheese and add it to the mixture too.
7. Coat the mixture with the silicone spatula.
8. Heat the air fryer to 375 F and cook the frittata for 15 minutes.
9. After the due time – move frittata in the serving plates.
10. Enjoy!

**Nutrition:** calories 202, fat 15, fiber 0.7, carbs 3.4, protein 15.1

# Liver Pate

**Prep time:** 10 minutes
**Cooking time:** 10 minutes
**Servings:** 7

**Ingredients:**

- 1-pound chicken liver
- 1 teaspoon salt
- 4 tablespoon butter
- 1 cup water
- 1 teaspoon finely ground black pepper
- 1 onion
- ½ teaspoon dried cilantro

## Directions:

1. Cleave the chicken liver roughly and place it in the air fryer tray.
2. And then peel the onion and dice it.
3. Pour the water in the air fryer tray and add the diced onion.
4. Heat the air fryer to 360 F and cook the chicken liver for 10 minutes.
5. After the due time – strain the chicken liver mixture to discard it from the liquid.
6. Move the chicken liver mixture into the blender.
7. Add the butter, finely ground black pepper, and dried cilantro.
8. Blend the mixture till you get the pate texture.
9. And then move the liver pate in the small bowl and serve it immediately or keep in the fridge.
10. Enjoy!

**Nutrition:** calories 173, fat 10.8, fiber 0.4, carbs 2.2, protein 16.1

# Scrambled Pancake Hash

**Prep time:** 7 minutes
**Cooking time:** 9 minutes
**Servings:** 7

## Ingredients:
- 1 teaspoon baking soda
- 1 tablespoon apple cider vinegar
- 1 teaspoon salt
- 1 teaspoon finely ground ginger
- 1 cup coconut flour
- 5 tablespoon butter
- 1 egg
- ¼ cup heavy cream

## Directions:
1. Mix together the baking soda, salt, finely ground ginger, and flour in the small bowl.
2. Take the separate small bowl and break the egg there.
3. Add butter and heavy cream.
4. Use the hand mixer and mix the liquid mixture well.
5. And then mix together the dry mixture and liquid mixture

together and slowly stir it until it is smooth.
6. Heat the air fryer to 400 F.
7. And then pour the pancake mixture into the air fryer tray.
8. Cook the pancake hash for 4 minutes.
9. And then, scramble the pancake hash well and keep cooking it for 5 minutes more.
10. When the dish is prepared – move it to the serving plates and serve only hot.
11. Taste it!

**Nutrition:** calories 178, fat 13.3, fiber 6.9, carbs 10.7, protein 4.4

# Meatloaf Cuts

**Prep time:** 10 minutes
**Cooking time:** 20 minutes
**Servings:** 6

## Ingredients:
- 8 oz. finely ground pork
- 7 oz. finely ground beef
- 1 onion
- 1 egg
- 1 tablespoon almond flour
- 1 tablespoon chives
- 1 teaspoon salt
- 1 teaspoon cayenne pepper
- 1 tablespoon dried oregano
- 1 teaspoon butter
- 1 teaspoon extra virgin olive oil

## Directions:
1. Beat the egg in the big small bowl.
2. Add the finely ground beef and finely ground pork.
3. And then, add the almond flour, chives, salt, cayenne pepper, dried oregano, and butter.
4. Peel the onion and dice it.

5. Place the diced onion in the finely ground meat mixture.
6. Use the hands to make the homogeneous meatloaf mixture.
7. Heat the air fryer to 350 F.
8. Make the meatloaf form from the finely ground meat mixture.
9. Coat the air fryer basket with the extra virgin olive oil inside and place the meatloaf there.
10. Cook the meatloaf for 20 minutes.
11. After the due time – let the meatloaf chill little.
12. Cut it and serve.
13. Enjoy!

**Nutrition:** calories 176, fat 2.2, fiber 1.3, carbs 3.4, protein 22.2

# Flax Meal Porridge

**Prep time:** 5 minutes
**Cooking time:** 8 minutes
**Servings:** 4

## Ingredients:

- 2 tablespoon sesame seeds
- 4 tablespoon chia seeds
- 1 cup almond milk
- 3 tablespoon flax meal
- 1 teaspoon stevia
- 1 tablespoon butter
- ½ teaspoon vanilla extract

**Directions:**

1. Heat the air fryer to 375 F.
2. Place the sesame seeds, chia seeds, almond milk, flax meal, stevia, and butter in the air fryer tray.
3. Add the vanilla extract and cook the porridge doe 8 minutes.
4. After the due time – slowly stir the porridge carefully and leave it for 5 minutes to rest.
5. And then move the meal ëin the serving small bowls or ramekins.
6. Enjoy!

**Nutrition:** calories 298, fat 26.7, fiber 9.4, carbs 13.3, protein 6.2

# No Bun Bacon Burger

**Prep time:** 10 minutes
**Cooking time:** 8 minutes
**Servings:** 2

## Ingredients:

- ½ tomato
- ½ cucumber
- ½ onion
- 8 oz. finely ground beef
- 4 oz. bacon, cooked
- 1 egg
- 1 teaspoon butter
- 2 oz. lettuce leaves
- 1 teaspoon finely ground black pepper
- ½ teaspoon salt
- 1 teaspoon extra virgin olive oil
- ½ teaspoon diced garlic

## Directions:

1. Beat the egg in the small bowl and add the finely ground beef.
2. Cleave the cooked bacon and add it to the finely ground beef mixture.

3. And then, add the butter, finely ground black pepper, salt, and diced garlic.
4. Mix it wellcarefully and make the burgers.
5. Heat the oven to 370 F.
6. Spray the air fryer basket with the extra virgin olive oil inside and place the burgers there.
7. Cook the burgers for 8 minutes on the each side.
8. And then, cut the onion, cucumber, and tomato finely.
9. Place the tomato, cucumber, and onion on the lettuce leaves.
10. When the burgers are cooked – let them chill until the room temperature and place them over the vegetables.
11. Serve the dish!

**Nutrition:** calories 618, fat 37.4, fiber 1.6, carbs 8.6, protein 59.4

# Bacon Omelette

**Prep time:** 10 minutes
**Cooking time:** 13 minutes
**Servings:** 6

## Ingredients:

- 6 eggs
- ¼ cup almond milk
- ½ teaspoon turmeric
- ½ teaspoon salt
- 1 tablespoon dried dill
- 4 oz. bacon
- 1 teaspoon butter

## Directions:

1. Beat the egg in the mixer small bowl and add almond milk.
2. Mix up the mixture with the help of the mixer until it is smooth.
3. Add the turmeric, salt, and dried dill.
4. And then cut the bacon.
5. Heat the air fryer to 360 F and place the cut bacon in the air fryer tray.
6. Cook the bacon for 5 minutes.

7. And then, turn the bacon into another side and pour the egg mixture over it.
8. Cook the omelet for 8 minutes more.
9. After the due time and the omelet is prepared – move it to the plate and cut into the servings.
10. Enjoy!

**Nutrition:** calories 196, fat 15.3, fiber 0.3, carbs 1.6, protein 12.9

# Egg Butter

**Prep time:** 10 minutes
**Cooking time:** 17 minutes
**Servings:** 4

## Ingredients:
- 4 eggs
- 4 tablespoon butter
- 1 teaspoon salt

## Directions:
1. Cover the air fryer basket with the foil and place the eggs there.

2. And then move the air fryer basket in the air fryer and cook the eggs for 17 minutes at 320 F.
3. After the due time – remove the cooked eggs from the air fryer basket and place them in the cold water to make them chill.
4. And then, peel the eggs and cleave them finely.
5. And then mix together the cleaved eggs with the butter and add salt.
6. Mix it welluntil you get the spread texture.
7. Serve the egg butter with the keto almond bread.
8. Enjoy!

**Nutrition:** calories 164, fat 8.5, fiber 3, carbs 21.67, protein 3

# Breakfast Coconut Porridge

**Prep time:** 10 minutes
**Cooking time:** 7 minutes
**Servings:** 4

## Ingredients:

- 1 cup coconut milk
- 3 tablespoon blackberries
- ¼ teaspoon salt
- 3 tablespoon coconut flakes
- 5 tablespoon chia seeds
- 1 teaspoon finely ground cinnamon
- 1 teaspoon butter
- 2 tablespoon walnuts

## Directions:

1. Pour the coconut milk in the air fryer tray.
2. Add the salt, coconut flakes, chia seeds, finely ground cinnamon, and butter.
3. Crush the walnuts and add them in the air fryer tray too.
4. And then coat the mixture with salt.

5. Mash the blackberries with the help of the fork and add them in the air fryer tray too.
6. Cook the porridge at 375 F for 7 minutes.
7. After the due time – remove the air fryer basket from the air fryer and let sit for 5 minutes to rest.
8. And then slowly stir the porridge carefully with the help of the wooden spoon and serve.
9. Enjoy!

**Nutrition:** calories 279, fat 24.6, fiber 9.1, carbs 13.3, protein 5.7

# Mushroom Omelet

**Prep time:** 10 minutes
**Cooking time:** 12 minutes
**Servings:** 9

## Ingredients:

- 1 tablespoon flax seeds
- 7 eggs
- ½ cup cream cheese
- 4 oz. white mushrooms
- 1 teaspoon extra virgin olive oil
- 1 teaspoon finely ground black pepper
- ½ teaspoon paprika to taste
- ¼ teaspoon salt

## Directions:

1. Cut the mushrooms and coat them with the salt, paprika to taste, and finely ground black pepper.
2. Heat the air fryer to 400 F.
3. Spray the air fryer tray with extra virgin olive oil inside and place the cut mushrooms there.
4. Cook the mushrooms for 3 minutes.

5. Slowly stir them carefully after 2 minutes of cooking.
6. And then, beat the eggs in the small bowl.
7. Add the cream cheese and flax seeds.
8. Mix the egg mixture up carefully until you get the smooth texture.
9. And then pour the omelet mixture into the air fryer tray over the mushrooms.
10. Slowly stir the omelet gently and cook it for 7 minutes more.
11. After the due time – remove the cooked omelet from the air fryer tray using the wooden spatula.
12. Cut it into the servings.
13. Enjoy!

**Nutrition:** calories 106, fat 8.7, fiber 0.4, carbs 1.5, protein 5.9

# Western Omelette

**Prep time:** 10 minutes
**Cooking time:** 10 minutes
**Servings:** 4

**Ingredients:**
- 1 green pepper
- ½ onion
- 5 eggs
- 3 tablespoon cream cheese
- 1 teaspoon extra virgin olive oil
- 1 teaspoon dried cilantro
- 1 teaspoon dried oregano
- 1 teaspoon butter
- 3 oz. Parmesan, minced

**Directions:**
1. Beat the eggs in the small bowl and whisk them well.
2. Coat the whisked eggs with the cream cheese, dried cilantro, and dried oregano.
3. Add minced Parmesan and butter and mix the egg mixture up.
4. Heat the air fryer to 360 F.

5. Pour the egg mixture into the air fryer tray and place it in the air fryer.
6. Cook the omelet for 10 minutes.
7. And then, cleave the green pepper and dice the onion.
8. Pour the extra virgin olive oil in the skillet and Heat it well.
9. And then add the cleaved green pepper and roast it for 3 minutes on the medium heat.
10. And then add the diced onion and cook it for 5 minutes more.
11. Slowly stir the vegetables frequently.
12. And then, remove the cooked omelet from the air fryer tray and place it on the plate.
13. Add the roasted vegetables and serve it,
14. Enjoy!

**Nutrition:** calories 204, fat 14.9, fiber 1, carbs 4.3, protein 14.8

# Keto Bread-Free Sandwich

**Prep time:** 10 minutes
**Cooking time:** 10 minutes
**Servings:** 2

## Ingredients:

- 2 cuts Cheddar cheese
- 6 oz. finely ground chicken
- 1 teaspoon tomato puree
- 1 teaspoon cayenne pepper
- 1 egg
- ½ teaspoon salt
- 1 tablespoon dried dill
- ½ teaspoon extra virgin olive oil

- 2 lettuce leaves

**Directions:**
1. Mix together the finely ground chicken with the cayenne pepper and salt.
2. Add the dried dill and slowly stir it.
3. And then beat the egg in the finely ground chicken mixture and slowly stir it well with the help of the spoon.
4. And then, make 2 medium burgers from the finely ground chicken mixture.
5. Heat the air fryer to 380 F.
6. Spray the air fryer tray with the extra virgin olive oil and place the finely ground chicken burgers there.
7. Cook the chicken burgers for 10 minutes. Turn the burgers to another side after 6 minutes of cooking.
8. After the due time – move the cooked chicken burgers in the lettuce leaves.

9. Coat them with the tomato puree and cover with Cheddar cuts.
10. Serve it!

**Nutrition:** calories 324, fat 19.2, fiber 0.5, carbs 2.3, protein 34.8

# Seed Porridge

**Prep time:** 7 minutes
**Cooking time:** 12 minutes
**Servings:** 3

**Ingredients:**
- 1 tablespoon butter
- 3 tablespoon chia seeds
- 3 tablespoon sesame seeds
- ¼ teaspoon salt
- 1 egg
- 1/3 cup heavy cream
- ¼ teaspoon nutmeg

**Directions:**

1. Place the butter in the air fryer tray.
2. Add chia seeds, sesame seeds, heavy cream, salt, and nutmeg.
3. Slowly stir it gently.
4. And then beat the egg in the mug and whisk it with the fork.
5. Add the whisked egg in the air fryer tray too.
6. Slowly stir the mixture with the help of the wooden spatula.
7. And then, Heat the air fryer to 375 F.
8. Place the air fryer tray in the air fryer and cook the porridge for 12 minutes.
9. Slowly stir it 3 times during the cooking.
10. And then remove the porridge from the air fryer tray immediately.
11. Serve it hot!

**Nutrition:** calories 275, fat 22.5, fiber 9.7, carbs 13.2, protein 7.9

# Diced Beef Keto Sandwich

**Prep time:** 11 minutes
**Cooking time:** 16 minutes
**Servings:** 2

**Ingredients:**

- 6 oz. diced beef
- ½ avocado pitted
- ½ tomato
- ½ teaspoon chili flakes
- 1/3 teaspoon salt
- ½ teaspoon finely ground black pepper
- 1 teaspoon extra virgin olive oil
- 1 teaspoon flax seeds
- 4 lettuce leaves

**Directions:**

1. Mix together the diced beef with the chili flakes and salt.
2. Add flax seeds and slowly stir the meat mixture with the help of the fork.
3. Heat the air fryer to 370 F.
4. Pour the extra virgin olive oil in the air fryer tray.

5. Make 2 burgers from the beef mixture and place them in the air fryer tray.
6. Cook the burgers for 8 minutes on the each side.
7. And then, cut the tomato and avocado.
8. Separate the cut ingredients into 2 servings.
9. Place the avocado and tomato on 2 lettuce leaves.
10. And then add the cooked diced beef burgers.
11. Serve the sandwiches only hot.
12. Enjoy!

**Nutrition:** calories 292, fat 17.9, fiber 4.1, carbs 5.9, protein 27.2

# Keto Spinach Quiche

**Prep time:** 15 minutes
**Cooking time:** 21 minutes
**Servings:** 6

## Ingredients:

- ½ cup almond flour
- 4 tablespoon water, boiled
- 1 teaspoon salt
- 1 cup spinach
- ¼ cup cream cheese
- ½ onion
- 1 teaspoon finely ground black pepper
- 3 eggs
- 6 oz. Cheddar cheese, minced
- 1 teaspoon extra virgin olive oil

## Directions:

1. Mix together the water with the almond flour and add salt.
2. Mix the mixture up and knead the non-sticky soft dough.
3. And then spray the air fryer tray with the extra virgin olive oil inside.

4. Set the air fryer to 375 F and Heat it.
5. Roll the dough and place it in the air fryer tray in the shape of the crust.
6. And then, place the air fryer tray in the air fryer and cook it for 5 minutes.
7. And then, cleave the spinach and mix together it with the cream cheese and finely ground black pepper.
8. Dice the onion and add it to the spinach mixture. Slowly stir it carefully.
9. Beat the eggs in the small bowl and whisk them.
10. After the due time and quiche crust is prepared – move the spinach filling in it.
11. Coat the filling with the minced cheese and pour the whisked eggs.
12. And then set the air fryer to 350 F and cook the quiche for 7 minutes.
13. And then reduce the heat to 300 F and cook the quiche for 9 minutes more.

14. Let the cooked quiche chill well and cut it into pieces.
15. Enjoy!

**Nutrition:** calories 248, fat 20.2, fiber 1.4, carbs 4.1, protein 12.8

# Morning Tender Chili

**Prep time:** 10 minutes
**Cooking time:** 10 minutes
**Servings:** 4

## Ingredients:

- ½ onion
- 8 oz. finely ground beef
- 1 teaspoon tomato puree
- 1 tablespoon dried dill
- 1 teaspoon dried oregano
- 1 teaspoon dried cilantro
- 1 teaspoon dried parsley
- 6 oz. Cheddar cheese, minced

- 1 teaspoon mustard
- 1 tablespoon butter

## Directions:

1. Dice the onion and mix together it with the finely ground beef in the small bowl.
2. Coat the mixture with the tomato puree, dried dill, dried oregano, dried cilantro, and dried parsley.
3. And then, add mustard and butter.
4. Mix the mixture up.
5. Heat the air fryer to 380 F.
6. Place the finely ground beef mixture in the air fryer tray and cook the chili for 9 minutes.
7. Slowly stir it carefully after 6th minutes of cooking.
8. When the chili is prepared – coat it with the minced cheese and slowly stir carefully.
9. Cook the dish for 1 minute more.
10. And then mix the chili mixture carefully again and move to the small bowls.
11. Taste it!

**Nutrition:** calories 315, fat 20.8, fiber 0.7, carbs 2.9, protein 28.4

# Chicken Casserole

**Prep time:** 15 minutes
**Cooking time:** 18 minutes
**Servings:** 6

**Ingredients:**

- 9 oz. finely ground chicken
- 5 oz. bacon, cut
- ½ onion
- 1 teaspoon salt
- ½ teaspoon finely ground black pepper
- 1 teaspoon paprika to taste
- 1 teaspoon turmeric
- 6 oz. Cheddar cheese

- 1 egg
- ½ cup cream
- 1 tablespoon almond flour
- 1 tablespoon butter

**Directions:**

1. Take the air fryer tray and spread it with the butter.
2. Place the finely ground chicken in the big small bowl and add salt and finely ground black pepper.
3. Add paprika to taste and turmeric and slowly stir the mixture well with the help of the spoon.
4. And then, minced Cheddar cheese.
5. Beat the egg in the finely ground chicken mixture until it is homogenous.
6. And then whisk together the cream and almond flour.
7. Peel the onion and dice it.
8. Place the finely ground chicken in the bottom of the air fryer tray.
9. Coat the finely ground chicken with the diced onion and cream mixture.
10. And then make the layer from the minced cheese and cut bacon.

11.  Heat the air fryer to 380 F.
12.  Cook the chicken casserole for 18 minutes.
13.  When the casserole is prepared – let it chill briefly.
14.  And then serve the chicken casserole.
15.  Enjoy!

**Nutrition:** calories 396, fat 28.6, fiber 1, carbs 3.8, protein 30.4

# Herbed Eggs

**Prep time:** 10 minutes
**Cooking time:** 17 minutes
**Servings:** 2

## Ingredients:

- 4 eggs
- 1 teaspoon paprika to taste
- 1 tablespoon cream
- 1 tablespoon chives
- ½ teaspoon salt
- 1 teaspoon dried parsley
- 1 teaspoon oregano

## Directions:

1. Place the eggs in the air fryer basket and cook them for 17 minutes at 320 F.
2. And then, mix together the cream, salt, dried parsley, and oregano in the shallow small bowl.
3. Cleave the chives and add to the cream mixture.
4. When the eggs are cooked – place them in the cold water and let them chill.

5. And then, peel the eggs and cut them into the halves.
6. Remove the egg yolks and add them to the cream mixture.
7. Mash it well with the help of the fork.
8. And then fill the egg whites with the cream-egg yolk mixture.
9. Serve the breakfast immediately.
10. Enjoy!

**Nutrition:** calories 136, fat 9.3, fiber 0.8, carbs 2.1, protein 11.4

# Crunchy Canadian Bacon

**Prep time:** 7 minutes
**Cooking time:** 10 minutes
**Servings:** 4

## Ingredients:

- ½ teaspoon finely ground thyme
- ½ teaspoon finely ground coriander
- ¼ teaspoon finely ground black pepper
- ½ teaspoon salt
- 1 teaspoon cream
- 10 oz. Canadian bacon

## Directions:

1. Cut Canadian bacon.
2. Mix together the finely ground thyme, finely ground coriander, finely ground black pepper, and salt in the shallow small bowl. Shake it gently.
3. And then coat the cut bacon with the spices from each side.
4. Heat the air fryer to 360 F.
5. Place the prepared cut bacon in the air fryer and cook it for 5 minutes.
6. And then, turn the cut bacon to another side and cook it for 5 minutes more.
7. When the bacon is prepared and get a little bit crunchy – remove the bacon from the air fryer and coat it with the cream gently.
8. Serve it immediately!

**Nutrition:** calories 150, fat 6.7, fiber 0.1, carbs 1.9, protein 19.6

# Kale Fritters

**Prep time:** 10 minutes
**Cooking time:** 8 minutes
**Servings:** 8

## Ingredients:

- 12 oz. kale
- ½ onion
- 1 tablespoon butter
- 1 egg
- 2 tablespoons almond flour
- ½ teaspoon salt
- 1 teaspoon paprika to taste
- 1 tablespoon cream
- 1 teaspoon oil

## Directions:

1. Wash the kale carefully and cleave it roughly.
2. The place the cleaved kale in the blender and blend it until smooth.
3. And then, dice the onion.
4. Beat the egg in the small bowl and whisk it using the hand whisker.
5. Add almond flour, salt, paprika to taste, and cream. Slowly stir it.

6. And then add the diced onion and blended kale.
7. Mix it welluntil you get homogenous fritter dough.
8. Heat the air fryer to 360 F.
9. Spray the air fryer tray with the extra virgin olive oil inside.
10. And then make the medium fritters from the prepared dough and place them in the air fryer tray.
11. Cook the kale fritters for 4 minutes from each side.
12. When the kale fritters are cooked – move them from the air fryer and chill.
13. Enjoy!

**Nutrition:** calories 86, fat 5.6, fiber 1.6, carbs 6.8, protein 3.6

# Keto Air Bread

**Prep time:** 20 minutes
**Cooking time:** 25 minutes
**Servings:** 19

- **Ingredients**1 cup almond flour
- 3 eggs
- ¼ cup butter
- 1 teaspoon baking powder
- ¼ teaspoon salt

## Directions:

1. Break the eggs into the small bowl and mix them up using the hand mixer.
2. And then melt the butter until the room temperature.
3. Add the butter to the egg mixture.
4. And then, add salt, baking powder, and almond flour.
5. Knead the smooth non-sticky dough.
6. Cover the prepared dough with the towel and leave for 10 minutes to rest.
7. And then, Heat the air fryer to 360 F.

8. Place the prepared dough in the air fryer tin and cook the bread for 10 minutes.
9. And then reduce the temperature to 350 F and cook the bread for 15 minutes more.
10. After the due time – check if the bread is prepared with the help of the toothpick.
11. Move the bread to the wooden board and let it chill.
12. And then cut the bread and serve.
13. Taste it!

**Nutrition:** calories 40, fat 3.9, fiber 0.2, carbs 0.5, protein 1.2

# Tuna Boards

**Prep time:** 10 minutes
**Cooking time:** 10 minutes
**Servings:** 4

- **Ingredients**6 oz. bacon, cut
- ¼ teaspoon salt
- ¼ teaspoon turmeric
- ½ teaspoon finely ground black pepper
- 6 oz. tuna
- 1 teaspoon cream
- 4 oz. Parmesan
- 1 teaspoon butter

**Directions:**

1. Take the air fryer ramekins and place the cut bacon there.
2. Place the small amount of the butter in each ramekin.
3. Mix together the salt, turmeric, and finely ground black pepper together. Mix it up.
4. And then shred Parmesan.
5. Cleave the tuna and mix together it with the spice mixture.
6. Place the cleaved tuna in the bacon ramekins.
7. Add the cream and minced cheese.
8. Heat the air fryer to 360 F.
9. Place the tuna boards in the air fryer basket and cook the dish for 10 minutes.
10. When the tuna boards are cooked – they will have little bit crunchy taste and light brown color.
11. Serve the dish only hot.
12. Enjoy!

**Nutrition:** calories 411, fat 28.3, fiber 0.1, carbs 1.9, protein 36.2

# Breakfast Cookies

**Prep time:** 10 minutes
**Cooking time:** 15 minutes
**Servings:** 6

- **Ingredients**½ cup coconut flour
- ½ cup almond flour
- 1/3 teaspoon salt
- 1 teaspoon baking powder
- 1 teaspoon apple cider vinegar
- 4 oz. bacon, cooked, cleaved
- 3 tablespoon butter
- 1 tablespoon cream
- 1 egg

**Directions:**
1. Beat the egg in the small bowl and whisk it.
2. Add the baking powder, apple cider vinegar, and cream.
3. Slowly stir it gently and add butter.
4. And then, add salt, almond flour, and coconut flour.

5. Coat the mixture with the cleaved bacon and knead the smooth, soft, and little bit sticky dough.
6. Heat the air fryer to 360 F.
7. Cover the air fryer tray with the foil.
8. Make 6 medium balls from the prepared dough and place the balls in the air fryer basket.
9. Cook the cookies for 15 minutes.
10. When the cookies are cooked – let them cool briefly.
11. And then move the cooked cookies on the serving plate.
12. Enjoy!

**Nutrition:** calories 219, fat 16.7, fiber 4.3, carbs 8, protein 9.8

# Chicken Hash

**Prep time:** 10 minutes
**Cooking time:** 14 minutes
**Servings:** 3

- **Ingredients**6 oz. cauliflower
- 7 oz. chicken fillet
- 1 tablespoon cream
- 3 tablespoon butter
- 1 teaspoon finely ground black pepper
- ½ onion
- 1 green pepper
- 1 tablespoon water

## Directions:

1. Cleave the cauliflower roughly and place it in the blender.
2. Blend it carefully until you get the cauliflower rice.
3. Cleave the chicken fillet into the small pieces.
4. Coat the chicken fillet with the finely ground black pepper and slowly stir it.
5. Heat the air fryer to 380 F.
6. Place the prepared chicken in the air fryer tray, add water, and cream and cook it for 6 minutes.
7. And then reduce the heat of the air fryer to 360 F.
8. Dice the onion and cleave the green pepper.
9. Add the cauliflower rice, diced onion, and cleaved green pepper.
10. Add the butter and mix the mixture up.
11. Cook the dish for 8 minutes more.
12. The mix the chicken hash carefully and check if all the ingredients are cooked.

13. Serve the chicken hash immediately.
14. Enjoy!

**Nutrition:** calories 261, fat 16.8, fiber 2.7, carbs 7.1, protein 21

# Chicken Strips

**Prep time:** 10 minutes
**Cooking time:** 12 minutes
**Servings:** 4

## Ingredients

- 1 teaspoon paprika to taste
- ½ teaspoon finely ground black pepper
- 1 tablespoon butter
- ½ teaspoon salt
- 1-pound chicken fillet
- 1 tablespoon cream

## Directions:

1. Cut the chicken fillet into the strips.
2. Coat the chicken strips with the finely ground black pepper and salt.
3. And then Heat the air fryer to 365 F.
4. Place the butter in the air fryer tray and add the chicken strips.
5. Cook the chicken strips for 6 minutes.

6. And then turn the chicken strips to another side and cook them for 5 minutes more.
7. And then, coat the chicken strips with the cream and let them rest for 1 minute.
8. Move the cooked chicken strips in the serving plates.
9. Enjoy!

**Nutrition:** calories 245, fat 11.5, fiber 0.3, carbs 0.6, protein 33

# Eggs in Zucchini Nests

**Prep time:** 10 minutes
**Cooking time:** 7 minutes
**Servings:** 4

## Ingredients

- 8 oz. zucchini
- 4 eggs
- 4 oz. Cheddar cheese, minced
- ¼ teaspoon salt
- ½ teaspoon finely ground black pepper
- ½ teaspoon paprika to taste
- 4 teaspoon butter

## Directions:

1. Grate the zucchini.
2. Place the butter in the ramekins.
3. Add the grated zucchini to make the shape of the nests.
4. And then coat, the zucchini nests with the salt, finely ground black pepper, and paprika to taste.
5. Beat the eggs in the zucchini nests and coat the eggs with the minced cheese.

6. Heat the air fryer to 360 F.
7. Place the ramekins in the air fryer basket and cook the dish for 7 minutes.
8. When the zucchini nests are cooked – let them chill for 2-3 minutes.
9. Serve the zucchini nests in the ramekins.
10. Enjoy!

**Nutrition:** calories 221, fat 17.7, fiber 0.8, carbs 2.9, protein 13.4